FOR THE LOVE OF SPORTS

SUMO

Jessica Coupé

AV2
www.openlightbox.com

Step 1
Go to **www.openlightbox.com**

Step 2
Enter this unique code
VKAXZL2KH

Step 3
Explore your interactive eBook!

AV2 is optimized for use on any device

Your interactive eBook comes with...

Contents
Browse a live contents page to easily navigate through resources

Audio
Listen to sections of the book read aloud

Videos
Watch informative video clips

Weblinks
Gain additional information for research

Slideshows
View images and captions

Try This!
Complete activities and hands-on experiments

Key Words
Study vocabulary, and complete a matching word activity

Quizzes
Test your knowledge

Share
Share titles within your Learning Management System (LMS) or Library Circulation System

Citation
Create bibliographical references following APA, CMOS, and MLA styles

This title is part of our AV2 digital subscription

1-Year Grades K–5 Subscription
ISBN 978-1-7911-3320-7

Access hundreds of AV2 titles with our digital subscription.
Sign up for a FREE trial at **www.openlightbox.com/trial**

FOR THE LOVE OF SPORTS

SUMO

CONTENTS

What Is Sumo?

Sumo is a form of heavyweight wrestling. It began in Japan more than 1,000 years ago. Japanese myths describe the first sumo match. It was between the god of thunder and the god of wind and water. The god of thunder won, and his followers inherited Japan.

As the years passed, sumo became associated with the Japanese Shintō religion. In 15th-century Japan, people would battle to entertain the gods of the harvest. They believed that if the gods of the harvest liked the wrestling match, they would give a good harvest.

Early sumo matches were held as part of harvest ceremonies.

The modern version of sumo tournaments began about 400 years ago. Wealthy Japanese men organized these events as a form of public entertainment. The tournaments were held at Edo, now Tokyo.

The purpose of the first sumo tournaments was to raise money for Shintō **shrines**. Over time, these events changed the sport. Sumo slowly gained the rules, **rituals**, and **ranks** it has now.

Today, **professional** sumo is known as Japan's national sport. There are about 600 active professional wrestlers, called **rikishi**, in several ranks. Many skilled sumo wrestlers come from other countries. These include Mongolia, Georgia, and Ukraine. This shows the increasingly international nature of the sport. **Amateur** sumo competitions are now held in many countries, including the United States.

Ryogoku, a district of Tokyo, is considered the home of sumo wrestling. The sport's most important stadium is found there.

The longest sumo match on record took place in 1954. It lasted more than 32 minutes.

The youngest wrestler to achieve the highest sumo rank was Kitanoumi Toshimitsu, at the age of 21 years and 1 month.

A top-ranked rikishi earns about $30,000 a month.

Getting Ready to Play

Sumo wrestling does not require much equipment. The most important item is the body. On average, sumo wrestlers weigh about 330 pounds (150 kilograms). This weight helps them win sumo bouts. Professional sumo wrestlers train all year to prepare for tournaments. They live in training centers called "stables." They train under retired sumo wrestlers.

In the sumo stable, wrestlers learn many different skills. Young wrestlers typically **apprentice** at 15 years of age. They grow their hair and wear it in a top knot called a chonmage. Wrestlers spend their time at the stable training, eating, and resting.

Before entering the ring, higher-ranked wrestlers wear a decorated apron called a kesho-mawashi. It is tucked into their sumo belt. The apron often is decorated with a national flag, the wrestler's **sponsor**'s product, or traditional symbols.

Sumo is performed in a ring, called a dohyo, on a raised platform. The platform is a circle made of partially buried rice-straw **bales**. It is about 15 feet (4.6 meters) in diameter.

When not practicing or taking part in matches, professional sumo wrestlers wear traditional Japanese robes.

A sumo wrestler wears a traditional sumo belt, or loincloth, called a mawashi. It is made from cotton or silk. Mawashi come in many colors. Lower-ranked wrestlers wear black. Female sumo wrestlers wear a leotard or similar clothing under their mawashi.

Sagari are decorative strips of cloth that hang down from the mawashi. They mark the area of the belt that is illegal to grab.

Professional sumo wrestlers wear traditional wooden shoes to and from their training stable.

The Sumo Arena

A dohyo is typically located in a large arena. Spectators may watch matches taking place from either box seats or raised stands surrounding the dohyo. Typically, a dohyo is made of tightly packed clay. It is covered with a thin layer of sand. The surface stands about 13 to 24 inches (33 to 61 centimeters) off the ground.

The rice straw bales around the dohyo are known as tawara. At the center of the dohyo are two parallel white lines, called shikiri-sen. These mark the starting position for the wrestlers. The wrestlers crouch behind the shikiri-sen before the match, or bout, begins. Once ready, they approach each other from there.

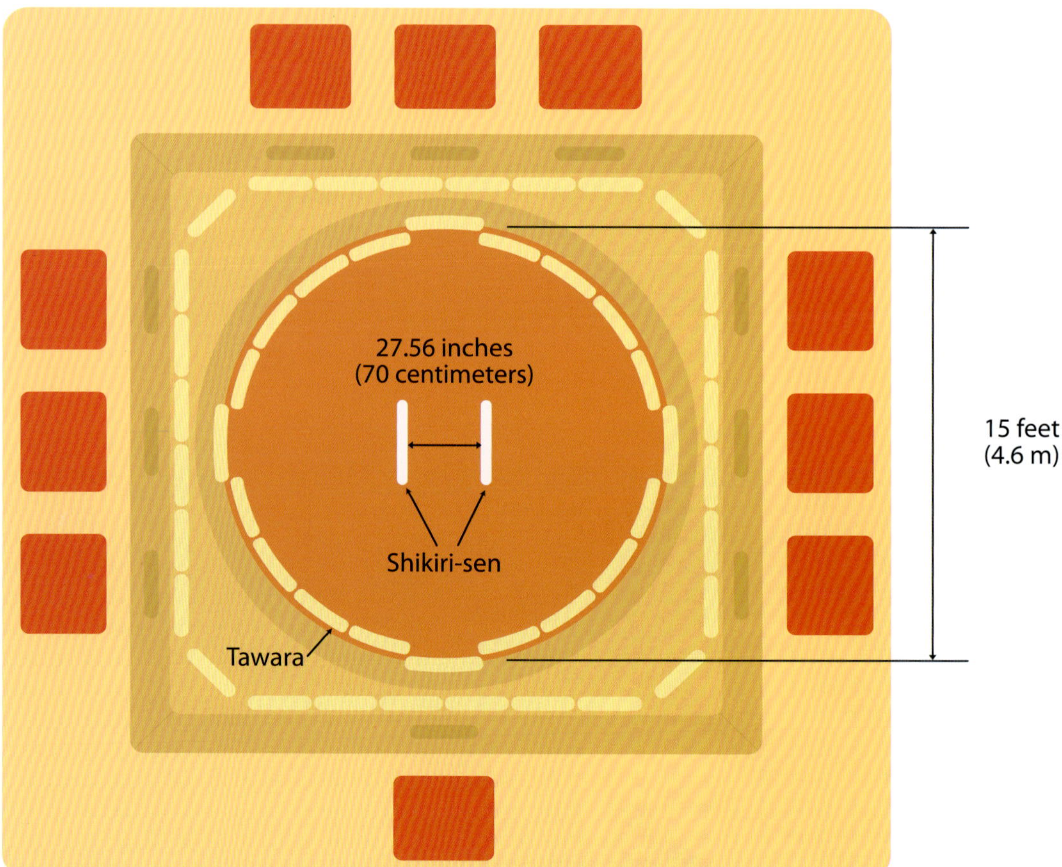

U.S. Sumo Open

The U.S. Sumo Open has been held since 2001. This makes it the world's longest-running non-Japanese sumo competition. It is also the first U.S. sumo event to include women's matches. At the 24th annual tournament in 2024, more than 4,000 fans attended.

Long Beach, California

The U.S. Sumo Open is held at the Walter Pyramid located on the campus of California State University, Long Beach. Today, the competition is broadcast on numerous sports channels as well.

Keeping Score

By winning matches, sumo wrestlers can increase their standing. Professional sumo wrestlers in Japan are divided into six different divisions. The money, privileges, and status wrestlers have all depend on their division.

The lowest division, Jonokuchi, has more than 50 wrestlers. Next is Jonidan, with more than 250 wrestlers. This is followed by Sandanme, which has about 200 wrestlers, and Makushita with 120. The second highest division is called Juryo. There are 28 wrestlers in this division. The top division is called Makuuchi. There are 42 wrestlers in this division.

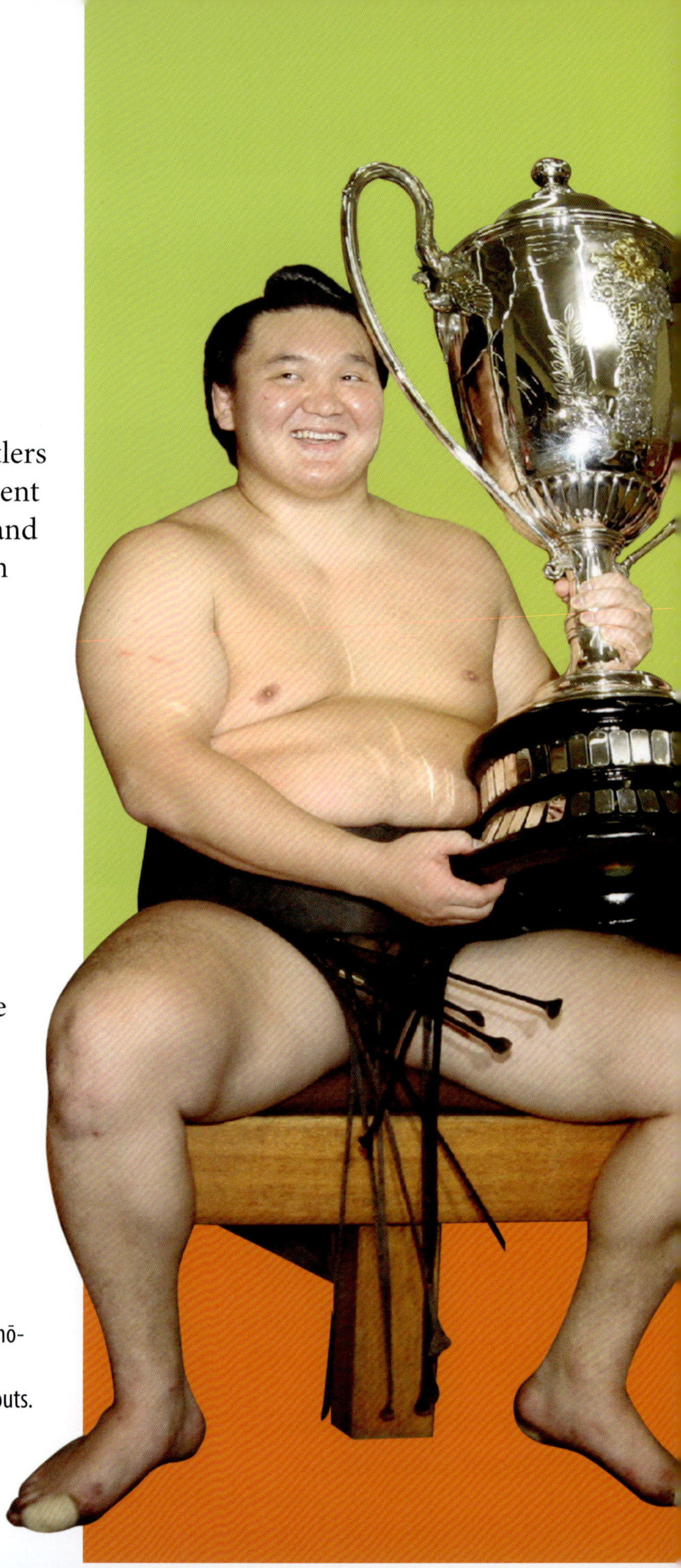

The best tournament result in professional sumo is called zenshō-yūshō. It means a wrestler went undefeated throughout all 15 bouts.

An official sumo tournament includes up to 15 bouts per wrestler. However, only Juryo and Makuuchi division wrestlers are allowed to compete in the maximum number of bouts. Before each major tournament, wrestlers are considered for promotion or demotion. This is based on their wins or losses in the previous tournament.

In an official tournament five judges, or shimpan, sit around the ring. They can overrule the referee, who is called a gyoji.

The word *makuuchi* means "inside the curtain." It refers to the curtained-off area where the top-ranked wrestlers traditionally sat before a bout.

Rules of the Game

In professional sumo wrestling, contestants perform several rituals before a bout begins. The opponents stand on opposite sides of the sumo ring, behind the shikiri-sen. Each wrestler throws salt into the ring. Many believe the salt will purify the ring and protect the rikishi from injury. Next, wrestlers will squat, raise their legs, and stamp the ground several times. This ancient tradition is meant to scare away evil spirits.

The bout itself usually takes only a few seconds. The goal of each rikishi is to force the other wrestler out of the ring. If a wrestler touches the ground with any part of the body other than the soles of the feet, he or she also loses the bout.

Using the arms to push an opponent out of the ring without grabbing the mawashi is known as an *oshidashi,* or "frontal push-out."

The rikishi depend on their strength and speed to win a bout. They use dozens of wrestling techniques to do this. These include flipping, tripping, or pushing the opponent out of the ring. Sumo wrestlers are allowed to sweep their opponents or lightly slap them. They may grab each other by the mawashi, making sure to only take hold of the legal area. Rikishi are also allowed to lift each other into the air.

Some moves are against the rules. For example, rikishi cannot pull an opponent's hair. Wrestlers are not allowed to punch, gouge, or kick their opponents. Breaking one of these rules means disqualification.

In addition to pushing, a sumo wrestler can win a match by throwing an opponent either out of the ring or on to the ground.

Sumo wrestlers often use tripping techniques to secure a win.

Playing the Game

Many people around the world participate in sumo wrestling. Most are amateurs who wrestle in amateur tournaments. The International Sumo Federation, the world's largest sumo organization, sponsors these amateur sumo wrestling events. Amateur sumo is available to anyone who wants to take part. These wrestlers do not have to join a stable and live the strict lifestyle of professional wrestlers. Today, people from about 80 different nations participate in amateur tournaments.

Any sumo wrestler who wins a professional tournament in Japan earns a replica of the Emperor's Cup. This silver trophy was donated by the country's emperor in 1926.

There are more than 80 techniques, called kimarite, that wrestlers can use during bouts.

The U.S. Sumo Association trains wrestlers in the United States. It also sponsors the U.S. Sumo Open tournament, which has become one of the largest amateur competitions in the world. Dozens of wrestlers from several countries come to the United States to participate in the event.

The Japan Sumo Association creates and maintains the rules of professional sumo wrestling. Only men are allowed to participate in professional tournaments. There are six tournaments held each year in Japan.

Three tournaments are held in Tokyo, in January, May, and September. Osaka has a tournament in March, Nagoya in July, and Fukuoka in November. Each tournament lasts 15 days. Rikishi compete in one bout per day.

The highest rank in the Makuuchi division is that of **Yokozuna**, or Grand Champion. Wrestlers become Yokozuna after moving up the ranks. Often they must win two tournament championships in a row. A Yokozuna cannot be demoted. As of 2025, there have only been 74 sumo wrestlers to ever earn the rank of Yokozuna.

When performing a throw, wrestlers may grab their opponent's belt, arm, or use their opponent's **momentum** to throw them.

The Tokyo sumo wrestling arena, Ryogoku Kokugikan, opened in 1985. Today, this huge stadium can seat more than 10,000 visitors.

History of Sumo

In the past, people in Japan practiced sumo wrestling to entertain the gods. Since then, sumo has become a professional sport. It is now known as the national sport of Japan. Today, sumo is practiced by amateur and professional sumo wrestlers around the world.

People from 88 countries participate in International Sumo Federation events.

1632 The legendary sumo wrestler Akashi Shiganosuke is said to be named the first Yokozuna.

1684 The Japanese government allows official sumo tournaments for certain reasons, such as charity. The first takes place at the Tomioka Hachiman Shrine, in Tokyo.

1925 The Japan Sumo Association forms to run professional sumo wrestling in Japan. It is overseen by the Japanese Ministry of Education, Culture, Sports, Science and Technology (MEXT).

1992 The International Sumo Federation is formed.

2001 The U.S. Sumo Open is created. This first tournament features 25 wrestlers from around the world.

2023 The U.S. Sumo Open includes 148 bouts. Sumo wrestler Phenom Mendee wins 27 matches.

In 1953, Japan became the first country to broadcast a sumo match on television.

Jesse Kuhualua, known as Takamiyama, was the first non-Japanese person to win a division tournament, in 1972. He was from Maui, Hawaii.

Hiyori Kon was one of the first women to gain recognition as a Japanese amateur sumo wrestler. She won the heavyweight division of the Women Junior World Sumo Championships in 2014 and 2015.

Superstars of Sumo

Sumo has seen many great professional athletes over its long history. Many sumo wrestlers have become famous for their speed and skill. Each professional rikishi is known by his "ring name."

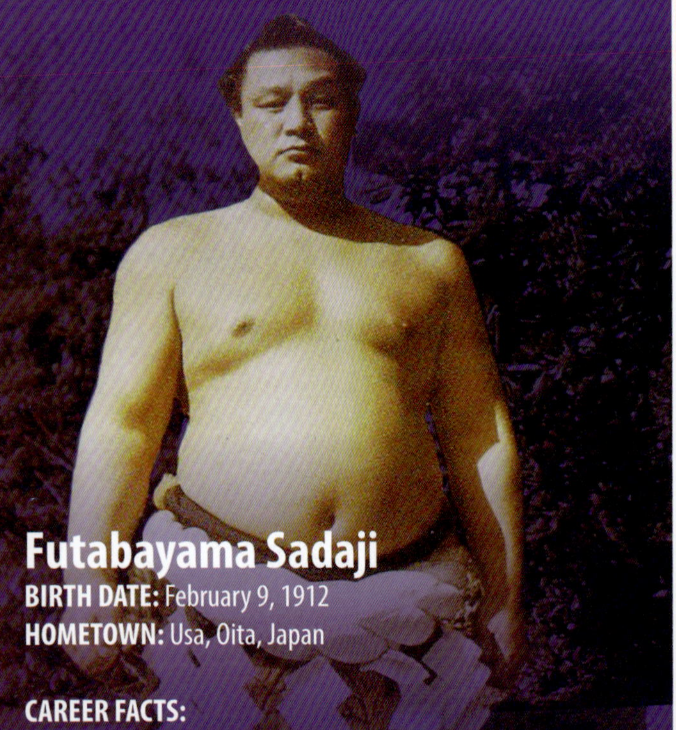

Futabayama Sadaji

BIRTH DATE: February 9, 1912
HOMETOWN: Usa, Oita, Japan

CAREER FACTS:

- Even though he was partially blind, Futabayama began training as a sumo wrestler at age 15.
- He defeated a Yokozuna when he was still a lower-ranked wrestler.
- In 1937, Futabayama became the 35th Yokozuna.
- Futabayama holds the record for the longest winning streak in sumo history, with 69 consecutive victories between 1936 and 1939.
- Futabayama was a member of the Japan Sumo Association from 1957 until 1968.

Taihō Kōki

BIRTH DATE: May 29, 1940
HOMETOWN: Sakhalin Island, Russia

CAREER FACTS:

- Taihō was the 48th Yokozuna.
- Taihō was the first sumo wrestler to win six tournaments in a row after World War II.
- Taihō was promoted to the rank of Yokozuna at the young age of 21 years and 3 months. He was the youngest wrestler to achieve this rank at the time.

Chiyonofuji Mitsugu

BIRTH DATE: June 1, 1955
HOMETOWN: Fukushima, Hokkaido, Japan

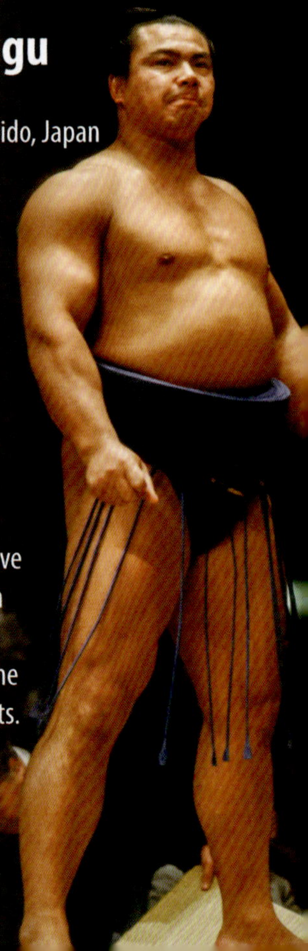

CAREER FACTS:

- Chiyonofuji won 807 matches in the Makuuchi division.
- Chiyonofuji served as the 58th Yokozuna.
- Chiyonofuji's longest winning streak was 53 bouts, the third-longest in sumo history.
- In 1989, Chiyonofuji became the first sumo wrestler to receive the People's Honor Award from the prime minister of Japan.
- In 1990, Chiyonofuji became the first wrestler to win 1,000 bouts.
- Chiyonofuji's signature move was the *yoriki*, or "frontal force-out."

Akebono Tarō

BIRTH DATE: May 8, 1969
HOMETOWN: Waimanalo, Hawaii

CAREER FACTS:

- Akebono started sumo wrestling professionally in March 1988, when he was about 19 years old.
- In January 1993, Akebono became the first non-Japanese person to achieve Yokozuna status.
- Akebono was the 64th Yokozuna.
- Between 1993 and 1994, Akebono won four of eight tournaments.
- In one tournament, Akebono won 14 of 15 bouts.
- When he retired in 2001, Akebono had won 566 individual bouts and 11 championships.

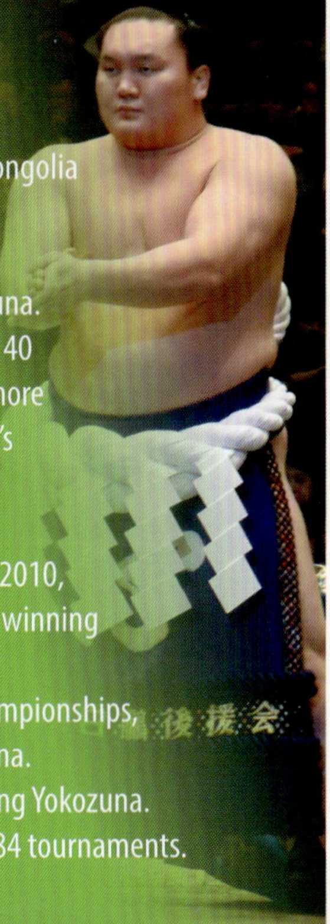

Hakuhō Shō

BIRTH DATE: March 11, 1985
HOMETOWN: Ulaanbaatar, Mongolia

CAREER FACTS:

- Hakuhō was the 69th Yokozuna.
- Hakuhō has won more than 40 Emperor's Cups and scored more than 1,000 victories in sumo's Makuuchi division.
- Hakuhō won 63 consecutive victories between 2009 and 2010, which is the second-longest winning streak in one calendar year.
- Hakuhō won 16 perfect championships, more than any other Yokozuna.
- Hakuhō is the longest reigning Yokozuna. He has been a Yokozuna for 84 tournaments.

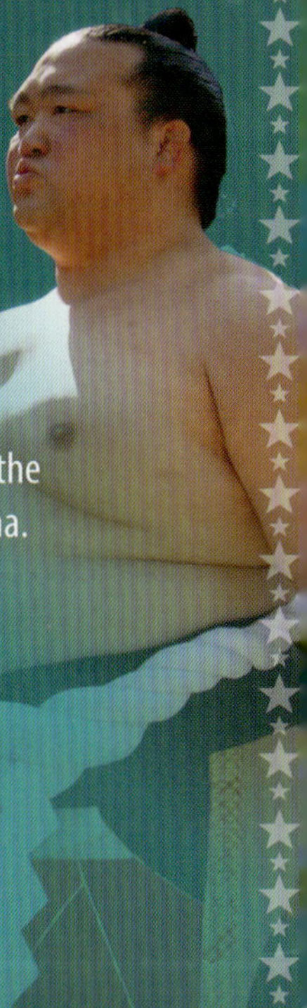

Kisenosato Yutaka

BIRTH DATE: July 3, 1986
HOMETOWN: Ushiku, Ibaraki, Japan

CAREER FACTS:

- In 2017, Kisenosato became the first Japanese-born wrestler in 19 years to gain the rank of Yokozuna. He was the 72nd Yokozuna.
- Kisenosato 's birth name was Yutaka Hagiwara.
- During his career, Kisenosato weighed about 390 pounds (177 kg).
- Kisenosato won his first Emperor's Cup in January 2017.
- In his career, Kisenosato had 800 wins and 496 losses.

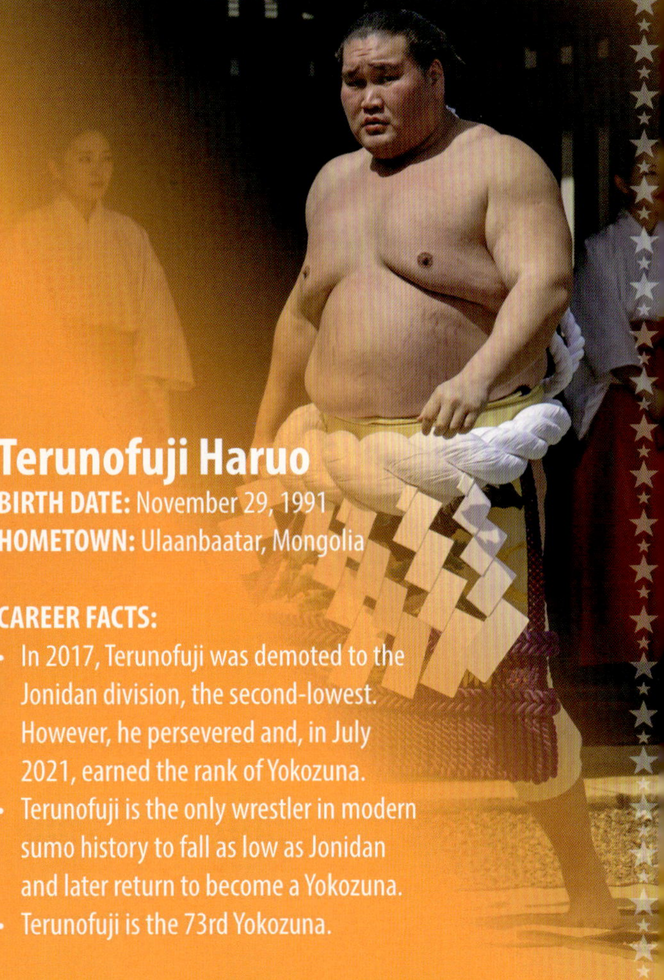

Terunofuji Haruo

BIRTH DATE: November 29, 1991
HOMETOWN: Ulaanbaatar, Mongolia

CAREER FACTS:

- In 2017, Terunofuji was demoted to the Jonidan division, the second-lowest. However, he persevered and, in July 2021, earned the rank of Yokozuna.
- Terunofuji is the only wrestler in modern sumo history to fall as low as Jonidan and later return to become a Yokozuna.
- Terunofuji is the 73rd Yokozuna.

Staying Healthy

Like all professional athletes, professional sumo wrestlers maintain their health through exercise and diet. Many wrestlers exercise for the first 5 hours of each day. They eat many vegetables that are rich in vitamins. Pasta and rice give them energy. Meat gives rikishi **protein** to help build their muscles.

Drinking water during the day is also important for sumo wrestlers. Water keeps their bodies hydrated and cool. Exercise, food, and water helps professional sumo wrestlers participate and win sumo tournaments.

After several hours of training, sumo wrestlers can lose up to 15 pounds (6.8 kg) of sweat. Drinking water replaces what they lose.

Eating a stew called chanko-nabe, which is high in protein and vegetables, helps give rikishi energy.

Strong, flexible muscles are important for sumo wrestling. Training their muscles every day helps sumo wrestlers prepare for tournaments. Stretching keeps muscles flexible. It is best to stretch during and after a warmup. Sumo wrestling warmup exercises include leg stretches and squats.

Sumo wrestlers have a number of daily exercises which help keep them fit and protect them from injury. One exercise, called shiko, involves raising one leg up, holding it for a second at the highest point, letting the leg down, and then squatting on the ground. Many sumo wrestlers do these leg lifts for at least 100 times in a row when exercising.

Sometimes, sumo wrestlers have sore joints after wrestling. They tape their joints to prevent injury.

THE SUMO QUIZ

- 1 -

When did sumo wrestling begin in **Japan**?

- 2 -

What is the name of the **belt** that sumo wrestlers wear?

- 3 -

How old are apprentice sumo wrestlers when they enter a sumo **stable**?

- 4 -

What was the name of the first **Japanese woman** recognized in amateur sumo wrestling?

- 5 -

In which year was the first U.S. Sumo Open **tournament** held?

- 6 -

Who was the first **non-Japanese person** to win a divisional tournament?

- 7 -

In a sumo **match**, what are wrestlers not allowed to **pull**?

- 8 -

How many **professional** tournaments are held in Japan each year?

- 9 -

What material is used to make the **dohyo**?

- 10 -

What is the **stew** that sumo wrestlers eat to get energy called?

ANSWERS: 1 More than 1,000 years ago 2 Mawashi 3 15 4 Hiyori Kon 5 2001 6 Jesse Kuhulua, also known as Takamiyama 7 Hair 8 Six tournaments 9 Clay covered by sand 10 Chanko-nabe

Key Words

amateur: doing something for enjoyment, not as a career

apprentice: to work under the direction of someone experienced in order to learn a sport or trade

bales: wrapped bundles made of a material such as hay

momentum: the force made by the weight and motion of something

professional: taking part in an activity or sport as a job

protein: complex compounds found in foods such as meat

ranks: in sports, a way of dividing participants into different positions within an organization

rikishi: a sumo wrestler

rituals: sets of actions done for ceremonial or religious reasons

shrines: places in which religious offerings are made

sponsor: a company that provides support to an athlete or team in exchange for advertising

Yokozuna: the highest rank in professional sumo

Index

Get the best of both worlds.

AV2 bridges the gap between print and digital.

The expandable resources toolbar enables quick access to content including videos, audio, activities, **weblinks**, **slideshows**, **quizzes**, and **key words**.

Animated videos make static images come alive.

Resource icons on each page help readers to further **explore key concepts**.

Published by Lightbox Learning Inc.
276 5th Avenue, Suite 704 #917
New York, NY 10001
Website: www.openlightbox.com

Library of Congress Control Number: 2025931420

ISBN 979-8-8745-2649-8 (hardcover)
ISBN 979-8-8745-2650-4 (softcover)
ISBN 979-8-8745-2651-1 (static multi-user eBook)
ISBN 979-8-8745-2653-5 (interactive multi-user eBook)

Printed in Guangzhou, China
1 2 3 4 5 6 7 8 9 0 29 28 27 26 25

012025
101124

Project Coordinator John Willis
Art Director Terry Paulhus
Layout Jean Faye Rodriguez

Photo Credits
Every reasonable effort has been made to trace ownership and to obtain permission to reprint copyright material. The publisher would be pleased to have any errors or omissions brought to its attention so that they may be corrected in subsequent printings. The publisher acknowledges Alamy, Getty Images, Shutterstock, and Wikimedia as its primary image suppliers for this title.